JAPANESE
SNOW MONKEYS

D1806026

PTW ©
Edutainment

Copyright © 2016 PTW Edutainment / PTW Photography

All rights reserved. No part of this publication may be reproduced, distributed, or transmitted in any form or by any means, including photocopying, recording, or other electronic or mechanical methods, without the prior written permission of the publisher.

www.puptheworld.com

EPILOGUE

Visiting the Snow Monkeys is an epic wild-life nature experience we recommend to anyone visiting or living in Japan. 300km north of Tokyo in Nagano Prefecture, it's an easy half day trip by train or 4 hours drive. We traveled there by Shinkansen (a Bullet-Train capable of going the speed of an airplane) combined with a couple of connector trains including the "Snow-Monkey Express". These trains provided insightful views of rural Japan, rice fields, farms and even Mt Fuji along the way.

Once arriving at Jigokudani Yaen Park, there was a 30 minutes bush walk through a snow covered forest valley, along a winding snow covered track. We could see the river and hear the waterfalls along the way. It is a beautiful ambient entrance.

You can enjoy an Onsen Hot Spring bath when you arrive, (a great way to warm up, relax and unwind from your journey) or you may prefer to go straight in to see the monkeys in the main monkey bathing area.

In arriving in the main monkey bathing area, you will be amazed by the antics of the monkeys. These creatures are super-cute and fun to watch bathing, chilling out, stumbling around, searching for food, and "piggybacking" each other. Surprisingly they can even roll snowballs, and throw them at each other (playfully). They are very peaceful, calm, gentle-natured monkeys who go about doing their own thing, mostly unfazed by the crowds of people that come to watch them.

HOT SPRINGS FOR HUMANS

There are a few hot springs designated for people, 5-10 minutes walk up the track at Kourakukan Ryokan just across the river.

These onsens are different to the "monkeys only" hot springs but occasionally monkeys will join people while they bathe (It's hard to keep them out). Have your camera ready!

These onsens are complementary for guests at Kourakukan Ryokan, and also available for 500yen (approximately $5) to anyone who wishes to indulge.

It's a Japanese custom to bathe naked at Onsens but at this Ryokan you're welcome to wear swimwear.

STAY THE NIGHT

If you're in no rush to leave, it is a marvelous experience to stay a night or two, enjoy the sunset, a peaceful evenings rest, and wake up revitalized and refreshed in an ambient peaceful valley, surrounded by snow monkeys.

It was a truly memorable experience to stay at this traditional Japanese multi-level guest house on the riverside. A cozy, family run Ryokan named Kourakukan just across the river a few minutes walk up the snow covered track from the main monkey area.

They provide a great bed and breakfast, a delicious full course dinner, and hot springs to bathe in.

We could see the snow monkeys from our room and enjoyed watching the monkeys from the Kourakukan's outdoor hot spring as we bathed.

TIPS FOR THE TRIP

- Be prepared for a 30minutes bush-walk. Snow covered ground can be extremely slippery.

- Take a walking stick to avoid injury. Some are provided free at the gate in limited quantities.

- Non-slip traction boots will stop you from slipping.

- Wear Waterproof Boots and take spare socks. The snow can be deep and the moisture will be absorbed by non waterproof boots. Wet shoes are uncomfortable.

- Wear waterproof clothing.

    Wet clothing can be extremely uncomfortable.

- Dress for the conditions.

    A warm hat, waterproof gloves, thick socks etc...

- Take an Umbrella. Snowfall can be intense. (On our second day there was a blizzard.)

- Prepare Snacks, Drinking Water, a Hot Drink in a Flask will help warm you up.

- Enjoy an Onsen while you are there. Hot springs are great in winter.

- It is recommended to avoid prolonged eye contact with the monkeys. (They may find it intimidating.) But... It may be hard not to stare at them, as they are fascinating kawaii creatures.

HOW TO GET THERE

The destination Jigokudani Yaen Koen is approximately 300km from Tokyo, Japan.

BY TRAIN

1) From Ueno in Tokyo to Nagano

      Bullet train, (Hokuriku Shinkansen) from Ueno Station to Nagano Station.

2) Nagano Station to Yudanaka Station

      (Nagano Dentetsu Line Limited Express Train)

3) Yudanaka Station - Kanbayashi Onsen gate

      We caught a Taxi (Buses are also available.) .

4) Bush Walk (approximately 2km) - to Jigokudani Yaen Koen

      30 minutes hike up and along a snow covered track.

BY CAR

If you prefer to travel by car, it is an estimated four hours drive from Tokyo.

GLOSSARY

Jigokudani: The name of the Park where this Valley of Snow Monkeys reside.
   Jigokudani literally means "Hell's Valley".

Kawaii: Cute, lovely, charming

Kourakukan: The name of the guest house, which also has its own private onsens

Nihon Zaru: Japanese Macaque/ Snow Monkey

Onsen: Traditional Japanese Hot Springs

Ryokan: A Traditional Japanese Guest House

Saru: Monkey

Shinkansen: Bullet-Train

ABOUT THE AUTHOR & PHOTOGRAPHER

"TEAMWORK MAKES THE DREAM WORK"

PTW is a Husband and Wife team with a Passion for Life, Travel, Creativity, and Adventures. Together they have traveled and lived abroad throughout many countries and cultures, gathering inspiration and documenting their experiences.

www.puptheworld.com
puptheworld@gmail.com
https://www.facebook.com/PTWEdutainment
https://www.instagram.com/ptwedutainment/